K-9 FLASH
BECOMES A HERO!

JASON K. JOHNSON

ILLUSTRATED BY KERRY WILLEY

SocialMotion
PUBLISHING

Published by Social Motion Publishing,
the first and only publisher in the
United States dedicated to social-impact books.
SocialMotionPublishing.com

First print edition

ISBN: 978-0-9704379-8-3

Produced in the United States of America

To anyone who has ever earned the title of K-9 Handler, I truly believe it is the most honorable profession in the world. To our four-legged heroes, I will dedicate my life to protect you for everything you have done for us. To K-9 Flash, who saved who? This book is dedicated to each of you.

—JJK9

This is the story of a police K-9 named Flash and how she went from not having a family or home to being one of the best police dogs in history.

As a one-year-old puppy, Flash lived on the streets all by herself. She wandered around in the cold, looking for food wherever she could find it. Flash didn't have any family, but she knew she was bound for greatness.

One day while she was walking the streets, trying to find something to eat, she was picked up by the dog-catcher and taken to the animal shelter.

Even though she had food and protection from the rain and cold, Flash did not like being locked up at all! She knew she would have to find some way out as soon as possible.

Then soon after, a police officer came to the animal shelter looking for puppies that wanted to become police dogs. Flash knew that being a K-9 was exactly what she was born to do. This was her big chance!

But not just any puppy can become a police dog. Flash had to pass many tests to prove she was smart, fast, and strong before she could enter the training academy. And she did, with excellent scores! Now it was time to meet her new human police partner, Jason.

When Flash met Jason, she knew she was going to like working with him every day. Flash enjoyed being at police dog school with all of her classmates, but most of all, she liked that she had a caring person who would take care of her and be a good buddy.

Because she studied very hard, it wasn't very long before Flash graduated from the academy and got her very own badge. She even got a police car with her name on it! Now she could go out on patrol with Jason to protect the families and children of her city.

Flash worked as a police dog for more than eight years and went on hundreds of calls. All of the bad guys were afraid of her because she helped put them in jail when they broke the law. She became known as the best K-9 that her police department ever had!

It was a sad day for Flash and Jason when she retired, because they would no longer work together. But she was now an older dog, and it was better for her to relax at home and not face danger. There was just one question. Where would she live? Police dogs don't always get to stay with their human partners when their work is done. Plus, the medical care and food from the police department stops. Just like when she was a puppy, she would have to be adopted again.

Luckily, she got great news. Jason could adopt her and give her a nice home! He could feed her, give her treats, take her out for exercise, and take her to the vet when she was sick. She was so happy and thankful for the good life she now had, especially compared to her days as a puppy all by herself on the streets.

But even though she was happy for herself, she wondered about the other police dogs. "What about the ones who worked hard just like me but don't have any medical care to help them in their old age?" That thought bothered her. Then she had a great idea.

Flash decided to start a project to help take care of police dogs that are too old or sick to work! She called it Project K-9 Hero and started looking for the first dogs she could help.

Very soon, Flash met a K-9 named Wesley. Wesley worked at the fire department with Captain Jennifer. His job was very important because he used his nose to help figure out if bad guys had started a fire!

Wesley and Jennifer were a great team and worked together at many big fires after the firefighters put the flames out. Wesley could find where the fire was started, and then Captain Jennifer could collect the evidence to help find the bad guy and put him in jail.

But now, after nine years at the fire department, Wesley was too old to work. Flash asked him to join Project K-9 Hero, which made Wesley's tail wag. Dogs like being helpful. He answered, "Yes!"

Flash was really happy she found Wesley because together they could help more dogs. The next K-9 they met was Ringo. Ringo worked for the state patrol for ten years with his handler, Trooper Paul. Their job was to find illegal drugs that bad guys were hiding in cars, houses, and all kinds of places.

They also visited schools and talked to kids about staying away from drugs and doing well in class. Ringo liked this very much because he loved children. But now that Ringo wasn't working anymore, he needed a new mission. Project K-9 Hero with Flash and Wesley would be perfect!

Flash, Wesley, and Ringo then met K-9 Kurt, who worked for the government in Washington, D.C. His human partner was Officer Joel.

Like Flash, Kurt worked for eight years, but Kurt's job was looking for bombs in cars and packages! He helped keep Washington, D.C. safe from bad people and was very good at his job. It was important work because he protected the Nation's Capital, where the President and members of Congress live.

When Flash told Kurt how she was trying to help other retired police dogs, Kurt was excited to be a part of Project K-9 Hero and joined her in her quest.

Now that Flash had Wesley, Ringo, and Kurt on her team, she knew she needed to raise money to help more retired police dogs all over the country. So she decided to visit as many people as she could and tell them about Project K-9 Hero. She also went to some big companies that might want to donate money for her cause.

Flash told everyone she met how important police dogs are and how they protect us to keep our families and neighborhoods safe. She learned that most people don't know how much money it takes to care for a retired police dog. Plus, most people don't know that the person who adopts the police K-9 pays this cost. But everyone agreed that, after the dogs' service to their country and sometimes risking their lives, they should get good care in their old age.

At one company where Flash told the story of Project K-9 Hero, the boss was so impressed that she gave Flash a big check as a donation. This money would be a huge help!

Flash was very excited to have Wesley, Ringo, and Kurt with her when the newspapers took photos. They were four really happy dogs! Now, together as a team, they could go out and find other retired K-9 heroes all over the United States to help.

Flash couldn't believe everything that was happening. Her idea for Project K-9 Hero had become something real. She discovered that a good idea plus hard work plus a team can accomplish great things. She now had a big new adventure ahead of her!

THE END

PHOTO ALBUM OF THE REAL K-9s FLASH, WESLEY, RINGO, AND KURT!

K-9 FLASH

04/26/2006

12/22/2005

01/05/2003

K-9 KURT

Kurt protecting the United States Capitol and other important places in Washington, D.C. ▶

Kurt enjoying a quiet moment in a park. ▼

K-9 RINGO

◀ Ringo loves meeting small children.

Oh, the strange places Ringo has to go! ▼

K-9 WESLEY

▲ Wesley with his human
partner, Captain Jennifer.

Wesley uses his nose to check
out a burned building. ▶

Remembering K-9 Wesley
May 29, 2002–September 20, 2016

by Fire Captain Jennifer Norton,
Wesley's handler

Wesley was trained at the Bureau of Alcohol, Tobacco, Firearms, and Explosives Canine Academy, where we met in 2004. He was an exuberant two-year-old with a nose that worked non-stop. Trained as an Accelerant Detection Canine team, we were one of only 50 in the country at the time and assisted fire investigators in solving crimes all over the western United States. We worked more than 200 fire scenes and arson investigations. He touched so many people in our community and acted as an ambassador for fire safety.

When Wesley turned 10, it was time for him to retire, but he had no trouble with his new leisurely life. He really enjoyed his food, swimming, and lots of love!

I am honored to have had the opportunity to work with Wesley as his handler for so many years. When he crossed the rainbow bridge, Project K-9 Hero was able to financially assist with his cremation and contribute toward a small memorial so that he will remain in the hearts of everyone he touched. All of this was possible because of the donations people have made to the foundation, and I am so grateful for their generosity.

ACKNOWLEDGMENTS

I truly appreciate each and every donor who has ever contributed to Project K-9 Hero, as well those who will donate in the future. We could not take care of our nation's four-legged heroes without your support.

A special thanks to Andrew Chapman at Social Motion Publishing for believing in me and my vision for this book. While Andrew made this book a reality, our illustrator Kerry Willey truly made it come to life through each illustration. Thank you, Kerry, for donating your time and talent to this project. I also thank all of my loyal, patient, and understanding friends and family. With your daily insight, honest critiques, and contributions, I feel confident that we are making the right decisions for this foundation as we move forward.

To you who bought this book, by purchasing it you have allowed me to follow my passion, and for that I thank you very much. I hope you've enjoyed this true story about my dog Flash and how Project K-9 Hero was founded.

Finally, thank you, Flash, for inspiring the following saying: "Save a dog's life, and they will change yours forever." This book and Project K-9 Hero exist because of you.

If you would like to help retired K-9 heroes like Flash, Wesley, Ringo, and Kurt, please visit our website at ProjectK9Hero.org and join me in "Protecting Those Who Protected Us."

ABOUT THE AUTHOR

Jason Johnson has a passion for police K-9s and has dedicated his life to training, working with, and taking care of them. He believes police K-9s perform selflessly for the departments and agencies they work for—but unfortunately, they are not offered proper respect in their retirement by those they served. It is Johnson's goal to change this through the foundation he started, Project K-9 Hero. (See more about the foundation on the next page.)

Outside of Project K-9 Hero, Johnson is a nationally recognized K-9 expert currently serving as a Field Canine Coordinator for the United States Government. In this role, he provides program oversight and subject-matter expertise to law enforcement and federal canine teams.

Prior to taking his current position, Johnson trained, instructed, and certified K-9 students in all of the top federal agencies and many other state and local departments; was the CEO of K-9 Solutions International; served in Iraq and Afghanistan as a top K-9 handler for a U.S. ambassador; served as a K-9 handler, trainer, and SWAT officer for two city police departments; served in the U.S. Army as a military police officer; taught as an adjunct professor at Henley-Putnam University; and earned his Master's Degree in Security Management from Bellevue University.

Johnson resides near Detroit, Michigan—with, of course, Flash right by his side.

ABOUT PROJECT K-9 HERO

Project K-9 Hero is a 501(c)3 non-profit organization that ensures the best quality of life for retired police K-9s and military working dogs. Its mission is to provide assistance with medical costs, food, and end-of-duty services for each dog in its program. Since there are no public funds for retired K-9s, the foundation relies on donors like you to fund its mission through generous contributions.

It is the goal of Project K-9 Hero to educate the public on the costs and responsibilities that occur after adopting a retired K-9 and ensure that each retired hero is rewarded with the way of life they deserve for their faithful and loyal service.

For more information, please check out the organization's website at www.ProjectK9Hero.org.

10061794R00020

Made in the USA
Middletown, DE
11 November 2018